T0353933

RUNNING AND TRIPPING IN HIGH HEELS

LISA L. BROWN, CFP®, CIMA®, MBA

authorHOUSE®

AuthorHouse™
1663 Liberty Drive
Bloomington, IN 47403
www.authorhouse.com
Phone: 833-262-8899

Published by AuthorHouse 10/21/2024

ISBN: 979-8-8230-3307-7 (sc)
ISBN: 979-8-8230-3308-4 (hc)
ISBN: 979-8-8230-3309-1 (e)

Library of Congress Control Number: 2024918289

Print information available on the last page.

CONTENTS

PREFACE

I do my best thinking when I'm running. It's quiet, so I have plenty of time to reflect. These reflections are often about personal stories that I've recently heard and how I would apply the experiences others have had to my own journey. Knowing how valuable it has been for me to internalize other people's stories and how they kept going after success or failure was what lead me to embark on this process of pulling together powerful stories from a diverse set of women and turning them into a mentoring book for early to midcareer women.

In January of 2022, I began working on my interview questions with the goal of finding dozens of professional and influential women who could speak about their journeys toward success. I wanted to learn how their experiences and mentors shaped them and what advice they would give to other professional women when they tripped, stumbled, picked themselves up, and forged ahead. I wanted to hear about the good and the bad, as we often learn more from our failures than our accomplishments.

The women in this book are CEOs and CFOs, entrepreneurs, top sales professionals, educators, retired executives, philanthropists, best-selling authors, and women continuing to climb the corporate ladder in their respective industries. I was blown away while collecting the words of wisdom from these professional women. In a few instances, I had a personal relationship with the women who contributed to this book, but in most cases, I met them for the first time when they graciously offered an hour or more of their time to sit down with me and open up like I never imagined. I was amazed, not only by many of their stories but also by how willing these strangers were to accept my request to be interviewed. In a world where it seemed like everyone was crazily running around with barely enough time to fit everything into their days, finding the time to share their stories appeared to be of the utmost importance to these women. These awesome women commented on how important they believed this type of project was to impact those coming after them and how, through a book like this, they could have an impact on women beyond their daily circles.

As I was wrapping up this manuscript, I happened to share one of the discrimination stories with a friend. My fourteen-year-old daughter, who was a freshman in high school, overheard our conversation. She looked at me curiously and piped in: "Mom, my teachers told me these things don't happen to women anymore. It's been fixed." She was referring to parity between men and women in the workforce. I was astonished. I calmly shared with her that discrimination against women in the workforce still happens. Perhaps we need more education about what it's like to be a professional woman today than I realized.

It's been a tremendous honor to learn from these women, and I am eternally grateful for their time and support. To protect privacy, pen names have been used. Company names are not shared, nor any derogatory comments made toward another person or employer. My wish for you is to pick up this book several times during your career and find the encouragement and strength to power through whatever obstacle you are facing. Please enjoy a walk through the lives of these strong women!

ACKNOWLEDGMENTS

With my deepest gratitude, I would like to thank the dozens of women who participated in my interview sessions and shared their profound personal experiences so that the women coming after them would have easier journeys. You are all my heroes, and I can't wait to watch what comes next for each and every one of you.

To my incredible daughters, Bella and Sophia. This book is as much for you as it is for other young women. I hope you'll read this one day and learn something that Mommy hasn't already taught you. There is so much life to live and so many experiences to be had. I can't wait to share in all of your ups and downs (you too, Corey!). As Jason Mraz's song "Have it All" goes, "may the best of your todays be the worst of your tomorrows."

CHAPTER 1

Early Influences

Education

Many people are taught by their parents that they can do anything and be anyone, but not everyone has heard this message. Trisha was raised to become a housewife and mother. When she told her mother that she wanted to go to college at eighteen, she was kicked out of the house. While showing her parents her first report card from college, which reflected straight As, her mother ripped it up.

It's hard to imagine parents being the roadblock to higher education. For many children, their parents are the ones who make that dream a reality or who consider attending college a table stake. But Trisha experienced the opposite and had to light that fire inside herself in order to persevere. She found a job that had a tuition-reimbursement benefit. This was necessary in order to put herself through college, since her parents were not supportive. Trisha is now in her thirties and has achieved the role of senior vice president of human resources. She is a wife and mother, juggling her corporate role with tenacity.

Social Norms and Money

Josephine also built a successful career in human resources for herself. However, unlike Trisha, her parents supported her mission. She grew up going to the office with her father and really enjoyed that environment. It helped her to know what direction she wanted to go in when she attended college— something in the business world. Ultimately, Josephine landed in human resources after obtaining her graduate degree. Trisha and Josephine are two successful women in the same field but with different degrees of difficulty getting there, and each was raised with varying expectations about social norms.

Like Trisha, several other women witnessed their moms being dependent on their dads for many things, including money. "I'm not going to rely on any man for money" was a common phrase shared by many of the women I interviewed. Some parents' marriages were tumultuous, and money was front and center for those difficulties. Claire's father was a hustler; her family always needed money. Growing up, she learned how to talk to anyone and sell anything from hot dogs to copiers on the street corner with her father. This experience caused her to always challenge herself and gave her the scarcity mindset. Claire went right from selling goods on street corners to landing a job in insurance sales, and she kept climbing.

As a child in Jamaica, Ashley had a comfortable life in her family's eight-bedroom house with a maid, nanny, and yard worker. At the age of eight, she and her family immigrated to the United States. As the Jamaican government limited the amount of money people leaving the country could take with them, she essentially went from rich to poor overnight. Ashley started working a paper route at age eleven, and from that point on, she largely became financially self-sufficient. As an immigrant, Ashely was taught that you don't come to the United States to "do average." She experienced sacrifice and worked her way out of the trenches.

Sophia's adventure-seeking career was influenced by her grandmother, who was one of the first female marines and an aviator in World War II. As Sophia grew up, her father saw her as gender neutral, so she did many traditional boy activities, like using a saw. Sophia spent eighteen years in the residential construction industry; at the time, 3 percent of people working in construction were women. Recently, Sophia launched a nonprofit to encourage and promote more girls and women to enter construction and trade businesses. Sophia recently became certified as a welder—once again not a traditional girl activity! Sophia's childhood and adult experiences do not conform to the societal norms for male and female roles.

Family Life

A tough childhood can be a great motivator to have a better life. Growing up, Virginia was one of four children. Her parents divorced when she was five. Her mother was overwhelmed by raising the children, and Virginia didn't witness her parents push themselves for a better life. She was a latchkey kid, going to college on the "free-lunch-kid scholarship." During her twenties, she got into running, and in her thirties, she started doing CrossFit. She hasn't stopped striving to achieve more. Virginia is now a communications coach and the CEO of her own practice. This latchkey kid wasn't raised to be a CEO, but she blazed her own path to the top.

Brooklyn was born in a slum just outside of Mexico City; her parents were fifteen years old. When Brooklyn was five, her family immigrated to Southern California. She never felt out of the ordinary, and she thrived as a track star, becoming one of the top student athletes in California. During her freshman year of high school, the family moved to Indiana, where there were "cornfields, farming, and white people," as Brooklyn put it. She was now different. Brooklyn learned she was undocumented, which made it harder to get into college in Indiana. She lost her purpose and became a teenage mom, having three kids before the age of twenty. Fortunately for Brooklyn, she came across some great mentors who saved her from dropping out of high school. They opened up opportunities in sales for her, and by the age of twenty-five, Brooklyn was making a six-figure income. Within a two-decade period, Brooklyn went from track star to almost dropout to sales star. Growing up, Brooklyn certainly did not have a silver spoon in her mouth or family role models who achieved professional greatness. But her story shows us that our pasts do not have to dictate our futures.

Sports and Business

Sports served as a common, positive theme among these successful women, like Virginia. Several attribute playing sports as a primary reason for being fearless and less worried about operating in a male-dominated professional environment or working with difficult male personalities. Carol believes playing team sports is instrumental in learning how to operate in the business world. There are many commonalities, such as working and winning as a team, failing together, developing leadership skills, and seeing what others have done to achieve success.

Leia was a competitive swimmer, which taught her time-management skills. She practiced before and after school. Krista played softball, which was the start of her competitive nature. Quinn ran in college and became a professional runner before entering the corporate world. Growing up, Sophia was the only girl on many sports teams; as an adult, she ran marathons. In high school, Sally tried out for every sports team but didn't make any of them. Yet her mantra was "effort counts," and she didn't forget that as she journeyed through the fields of public relations, event planning, and marketing. Kate felt that participating in team sports as a child taught her how to work with others and develop herself beyond what she thought she was capable of.

Sports also got these women through some tough times. When Isabel was eleven, her mom died tragically after having an allergic reaction to a piece of food at the dinner table. Isabel threw herself into tennis, which helped her manage those turbulent adolescent years. Maya played basketball in college and traveled all over the country. She knew this was important to her father. However, her mother was diagnosed with pancreatic cancer while Maya was in college, passing away four months later. Maya regretted not taking time off from basketball to spend with her mother, but basketball gave her an outlet during a challenging time. It continued to be an outlet during her working years. About ten years ago, Maya was working on Wall Street. A group of her male colleagues put together a basketball team to play in a summer league. She signed up. One male colleague pulled her aside and said, "You shouldn't play. It's for the guys, and you will get hurt." Maya knew she needed to push back on this. She made the cut as one of the top five players, becoming a star on the team. And no, Maya didn't get hurt. Her athleticism earned her a level of respect off the court.

Playing sports is exercise, and while the types of exercise we get as adults can be different from our childhoods, many of the women I interviewed say that exercise is one of their daily nonnegotiable activities. It gets them through the day, both mentally and physically, and allows them to take a more balanced approached to life. Keep playing sports and exercising as long as you physically can.

CHAPTER 2

Trail Angels

There are big lessons to be learned if you have your eyes open. For many women, their professional journeys took twists and turns, starting with their first real jobs in their twenties. Their chosen professions—or the people they thought they should be—were not always where they eventually landed, and that is OK. Sometimes you need to try, fail, and try again to find the right career. Along the way, you also need to listen to your "trail angels" when unexpected guidance and support comes your way. Trail angels are people who you encounter for a brief moment in time or for a season of your life and who provide you with valuable feedback or guidance that changes the course of your future. You may not even recognize that they were a trail angel until many years later, when you reflect on where you are in life and how you got there.

As a child, Elizabeth wanted to be a teacher. Her mom wanted her to be a doctor. Her dad wanted her to be an accountant. Elizabeth listened to her father and went to college for accounting. But she hated it and dropped out. Needing to work, Elizabeth tried different roles, including insurance and retail sales. Her boss at the insurance agency was one of Elizabeth's trail angels when he said, "You are too smart to be here. Go back to college and get your degree, so you can be the person you were meant to be."

It wasn't until Elizabeth lived overseas for her husband's career that she got into education. She began teaching cooking classes for nannies of American expatriate families in Thailand and Singapore. When Elizabeth and her husband moved back to the US in her forties, she got her teaching degree, her master's degree, and finally her doctorate. The variety of these experiences in her twenties and thirties were necessary for Elizabeth to ultimately find her twenty-five-year path as an educator. Later in life, when her mom was in a nursing home, Elizabeth was able to say, "Mom, your daughter is finally a doctor." This was a multidecade journey that started when someone challenged Elizabeth to achieve greatness early on.

Virginia began her career in health care by working with patients who had suffered brain injuries. It was a job where she "put people back together." This translated into her desire to become a coach. One of her patients encouraged Virginia to become an entrepreneur and start her own coaching practice. She followed that advice, becoming the CEO of her coaching business. We often don't think of our patients or customers as investing in us when we are focused on serving them. Yet our customers can be trail angels, and we need to be open to their guidance. It can be life-altering.

Isabel got her degree in marketing and found an opportunity to get into sales at a large organization. Her husband was in sales, and she was subtly competing against him for the title of who was more successful. When presented with an opportunity for a more senior sales role, Isabel declared to her boss, "I don't want to say yes to you and fail."

He replied, "What if you don't fail?"

That began the most rewarding year of her career. Isabel attained President's Club status, clobbering her sales goals and making her mark on this large organization. She needed to have her eyes and ears opened to this different opportunity in order to land on a successful career path. Perhaps it was her inner competitive spirit, yet had it not been for a superior having faith in her, Isabel may not have taken that leap.

At age fourteen, Brooklyn started working at a fast-food chain to help buy clothes for school and pay house bills. She had a regular customer who recruited her to work at a wholesale grocery store, managing a team of twelve people. A customer of this grocery store saw how hard Brooklyn worked and offered her a job in sales at a bank. Over a five-year period, Brooklyn went from working at a fast-food restaurant to closing multimillion-dollar deals, all because trail angels took an interest in her and her work ethic. They saw something special in Brooklyn, perhaps before she realized she had this potential.

Sometimes we encounter ditches alongside our trails. Krista wished she had listened more early on in her career. She would argue with people until they gave into her. She learned she could out argue anyone and get her way, but that rubbed people wrong. Gradually she learned the glory of having the idea without needing recognition for it. For all the bridges that Krista burned early on in her career, she'd like to find those former colleagues and tell them she's changed.

During one of Sally's first professional interviews she was told, "There is no way you are ever going to work here." It felt like a ditch. After being told never, Sally didn't land that job, but she did walk away with something more valuable—three tips on how to get more polished. That advice has paid dividends over the course of Sally's career.

If you hear the word *no*, especially early in your career, it's easy to assume that person is right because they have more experience than you. Don't believe it. You know yourself better than anyone else. Maybe you don't have the skills or chutzpah right now, but you can work toward any goal you set for yourself. If you hear the word *no*, be sure to ask *why*. Be open to feedback. Be inquisitive as to the guidance that person may be willing to share with you. It's one perspective, not the only perspective. Keep asking for feedback until it's polite to end the conversation.

Did you miss your trail angels?

You don't want to find yourself, later in your career, questioning whether there were trail angels who you missed. Josephine's path has been straightforward—a little too straight. After attaining her undergraduate degree, she moved into a master's program, then immediately started working in human resources. Almost three decades later, she is still in human resources. However, looking back, she wishes she had tried something else during the first five to ten years of her career. Perhaps there was a missed opportunity or a door that she could have opened but didn't. Josephine asked, "How do we expect kids or college students to know what they want to do the rest of their lives?" At some point, you can get so far into your career that it can be hard to make a change; you're not as nimble as you were in your twenties or thirties. You may have missed your trail angels.

Do you know someone who has spent their entire career at the same company? They usually don't have an active LinkedIn profile, know any recruiters, or have mentors outside their company. Perhaps they've thought about it but, not seeing the immediate need or benefit, pushed that to-do item to the bottom of their list. Why bother? They think they know everyone they need to know to be successful right there at their company. They aren't putting themselves in a position to be influenced by a trail angel. Navigating office politics in order to climb the ladder is not the same as building and fostering relationships outside your current employer. One day, management at your current company may deliver shocking news—your role has been eliminated. Then you will be in a scramble. How are you going to get another job? Who can help you? Where do you start? Where are your trail angels?

If you had been networking outside your company regularly, the process of getting your name and resume out there wouldn't feel so daunting. People around you often have a surprising ability to help you. Don't be afraid to ask for help. For example, ask, "Can you introduce me to your friend Janessa who is a manager at XYZ Company? I'd like to learn more about their open sales manager role."

Don't assume that person will jump through hoops to help until you've at least proven yourself worthy of their support on some level. After all, why should they lay their reputation on the line for you? Ask them to lunch. Do your homework. Find common ground. Build the relationship. First impressions can also be last impressions. But if you do this right, perhaps you will find your trail angel before they find you. People will be in your life for a reason or a season. Honor and learn from those around you, as you never know how your future will be shaped by those relationships.

CHAPTER 3

We All Make Mistakes

We all make mistakes. After all, that is the premise for tripping in high heels! None of us are perfect, nor do we have flawless resumes. Some blunders are small, while others are massive. All of these women have made mistakes and recovered from them. So will you. How you pick yourself back up and learn from your mistakes is more important than making the mistake, as many of these women experienced.

Carmen was the vice president of finance operations and in a leading role for taking a company public. She offered to manage the initial public offering process, as her team was running hard and fast to get the deal closed by year's end. She had hired an accounts payable person who ended up being horrible. Several financial items did not get uploaded in time, and they couldn't close the deal by year's end. This person was replaced by an excellent candidate who discovered $1 million worth of invoices were never approved during the prior person's time there. Carmen felt like she had been punched in the gut. She had to break this news to the board of directors. After that night, Carmen went home and slumped in her chair. That wasn't the only $1 million mistake she encountered during her career. When working in Upstate New York, she wired $1 million to the wrong company. All five checkpoints had been missed in that transaction. As a result of her experiences and mistakes, Carmen calls herself a root analysis person. She asks, "What happened and how do we fix it going forward?" Carmen will tell you that if you think you won't have missteps in your career, you're wrong.

At this point in her career, Claire feels like she has made not one royal mistake but several small ones along the way. Once she realizes she's messed up, Claire jumps all over fixing it. After a request for proposal didn't go well, she took a few days to process what went wrong and concluded that she had not prepared enough. The blame could easily be placed on someone else, yet a true professional will look at their individual contributions in the process or lack thereof. Through sales coaching, Claire has learned to focus on the activity and the process, not the outcomes. Claire is a top performer in her company and is often interviewed by national media. "The success came from the journey of getting there."

"I blew up my career," Josephine recalls of working at her financial services company. There was a new chief human resources officer who was a "huge suck up." Josephine could not control her feelings of distaste for this person. She said some things that didn't sit well with her boss, and she knew he was waiting for her to leave on her own. Many of her peers thought she was crazy to quit. Josephine knew she could've played the game better and even gotten a promotion, but she didn't go in that direction.

Hearing this story, you could argue that you shouldn't work for a boss you don't respect. Ask yourself the following questions:

Am I being short sighted? Am I so set in my ways that I'm not willing to try to understand the other person's perspective? After being honest and objective with yourself, give it time. Then make your final decision. If it isn't working out or if you can't be yourself at work, maybe it's time to move on, like Josephine did. However, she didn't leave blindly. Josephine secured a severance package before exiting.

Early in her career, Ashley had a female boss who she did not care for. Instead of working through her issues and concerns, Ashley took a scorched-earth approach. She didn't know the important lesson of never making enemies at the time. Now she describes her past self as inelegant, unkind, and thoughtless about the long game. Ten years later, Ashley ran into her old boss at a job interview. She happened to be one of the people interviewing Ashley for the job. The woman's best friend ended up being Ashley's superior. Her prior scorched-earth approach felt like a negative that kept coming back to haunt her, and she didn't know when it would end.

If you ask Elizabeth about how to handle mistakes, she'll ask you if there is blood. "If not, then keep moving." She encourages you to keep moving forward when you fall. Sometimes it's a few steps, and sometimes it is a mile. So how do you overcome making a mistake? In 2021, the *Harvard Business Review* addressed this issue with the following list of proactive steps.

1) Be proactive. Once you become aware of the mistake, get in front of it before the situation escalates.
2) Offer an apology. Make it genuine and acknowledge your error and the harm it caused to another person, team, or the business. Be humble; don't be defensive. Don't use the word *if* in your apology, as it doesn't show ownership of your mistake. For example, the phrase "if I had more

information about the accounting process, the payment would have been processed on time" could be rephrased to "I am sorry that I made a mistake processing the payment and that this damaged the relationship with our large customer. I have reviewed the procedures manual, understand what I did wrong, and now have the process documented next to my computer."

3) Make amends with those impacted. Show how you have corrected your behavior and commit to not making the mistake again. Your words need to match your actions going forward.

4) Show your boss that you are making progress. Find ways to position yourself in front of people in order to show the progress you have made, rebuild trust, and shift perceptions. People tend to remember your faults more than your strengths, so turn the narrative around. It can take time to rebuild trust and perceptions, so be patient.

5) Have compassion for yourself and others. When you make a mistake, treat yourself like you would a friend in a similar situation. To help ensure your mistake becomes a valuable learning experience, understand how you can prevent the mistake in the future and think of a lesson from this experience that you can commit to memory. If you learn how to forgive yourself and move forward, you will be more able to show compassion to others who make mistakes that impact you in the future. None of us are perfect.[1]

---

[1] Dina Denham Smith, "You Made a Big Mistake at Work. What Should You Do?" *Harvard Business Review*, November 5, 2021, https://hbr.org/2021/11/you-made-a-big-mistake-at-work-what-should-you-do.

CHAPTER 4

Career and Financial Coaching Tips

The women in this book have expansive backgrounds, and collectively, they bring an array of wisdom to all of us. What follows is a summary of the top career advice these women shared during their interviews, based on their personal experiences. I've divided these tips into the six most common topics shared with me. Much of this advice came from these women going through a difficult time and coming out the other side in a better place. There will be times when this advice will resonate. Other times, perhaps you'll disagree. That's understandable, as your career experiences will be unique.

Following the career coaching tips, I've included a list of financial coaching tips, which are based on my decades of experience in providing financial advice to busy corporate professionals. Some of the most satisfying moments in my career have been telling clients, "You have enough money to walk away today." Especially if they find themselves unhappy with their current job, boss, colleagues, or work environment, knowing they don't have to be a punching bag is completely freeing to the person who hears that good news.

Write down your own coaching tips at the end of this list. Keep adding to the list as you grow in your career.

Career

The Right Job

- Get the right job so that you can enjoy your work. If you are miserable, you are not likely to meet expectations.
- When interviewing for a job, ask value-based questions rather than job-related questions. For example, you could say, "Tell me about the culture within this company and how you see that being brought to life. Show me what happens at this company when bad things occur, such as _____."
- Try to figure out the character of the people you'll be working with and always know who your boss will be.
- If you put your heart into your job, it can suck the life out of you. Consider getting your pats on the head in other parts of your life. If self-validation happens at your job, that's just a bonus.
- Once you've been in a job for ten years, people wonder if you are a one-trick horse and can still adapt to change.
- You don't need to stick with a company or job for ten years. Get things running. Then turn it over to others to lead. Have an exit strategy. Be clear on your role and your time frame.
- Stop feeling like you have to stay in the same industry. You do not have to go backwards to switch industries. Don't be afraid to pivot.

It's Your Time

- Control your time and create space to be creative. Schedule time to focus.
- Set aside time to work *on* the business rather than in the business.
- It's OK to say no.
- Set your boundaries early on in your career and in a new job rather than try to change habits or what people expect of you later on. For example, if you start a job and are always working during your vacations, people will expect that they can and should reach you when you're taking time off.

Seek Help

- When you are not sure what to do next with your career, reach out to ten people to do a mock interview.
- Ask for regular feedback. Don't wait for your performance review, because, by then, it might be too late.
- Get a life coach. This can be a game changer.
- Work with a counselor. The best time to engage one is after you have gone through a difficult situation, when you are doing better.
- Tell everyone your goals. Someone can help you.

Lead

- Leaders lead people. They need to trust people. As a leader, you don't have to know it all.
- Corporate America is a "good ole boys club." The real discussions happen on the golf course.
- When you are in the C-suite, people will start gunning for you. Watch your back.
- In business, always focus on the red (the opportunities

to improve) rather than celebrate the green (the wins). If we are not failing enough, we are not challenging ourselves enough.

- Learners are earners.
- Luck is the confluence of preparation and opportunity. A lot of people are prepared but don't get the opportunity. Others have the opportunity but aren't prepared.

Be Strong

- An aggressive female will be remembered; a quiet one won't. Ask for what you want and what you need.
- Take risks, which is atypical for females. Eva shares, "As women, we feel like we need to have everything buttoned up before taking risks."
- Remove the word *hope* from your vocabulary. Hope stops you from taking action.
- You've got to be you, but people need to be able to relate to you. Know how to fit in with your peers, which may include participating in social activities.

Don't Be a Know-It-All

- When you are young, you think whatever is happening now is the biggest thing. The true challenges down the road will be bigger.
- Never say, "I told you so." Let people learn from their own mistakes.
- Do not vocalize your complaints.

Financial

Save Early and Often

- As soon as you get your first job, save at least 10 percent of your pay into your company's 401(k) or other retirement plan. Keep increasing that percentage by the amount of each raise you get annually, until you are putting in the maximum the IRS allows. For 2024, that figure is $23,000 if you are under the age of fifty and $30,500 if you are fifty or over.
- Always, always have a cash emergency fund. As you start your career, work to build a three-to-six-month living expense reserve in cash and quickly replenish it if you ever need to tap into it for true emergency purposes. For example, if your monthly bills are $5,000, you should have $15,000–30,000 of cash in the bank. A girls' weekend getaway is not considered an emergency for financial planning purposes!
- The higher you climb on the corporate ladder, the larger your emergency fund should become. For more senior roles, target at least twelve months of living expenses as your cash reserve or the amount equal to your noncompete clause at a minimum. Never let your emergency fund fall below three months.

Don't Tie Your Personal Wealth to Your Company's Performance

- Company stock grants are common in aligning employee behavior with company performance. The more your wealth is tied to your company or your company's stock price, the riskier your personal wealth becomes. Having a large concentration of your wealth tied to one company can build your balance sheet quickly, but if the stock price goes the wrong way, it can ruin your financial trajectory. Plus, if your paycheck is coming from the same company that your wealth is tied to, you can quickly find all your eggs in one basket.

- Have a plan to diversify your company stock grants once they vest. Make sure it's part of a disciplined plan that makes sense for your personal situation.

Minimize Your Fixed Expenses and Avoid Lifestyle Creep

- Big mortgages, car payments, private school tuition, hired help, and the like are part of your fixed monthly expenses. You probably didn't start your career with all this "stuff," but it can become part of your life very quickly if you don't watch yourself. As you climb the corporate ladder and make more and more money, keep your lifestyle in check. It's easy to think the good money will last forever. That's not always the case. Layoffs and firings happen. Relocations occur. Family members, including you, get sick.

- Having a lot of bills to pay each month puts added pressure on staying in a high-paying job. What if you fall out of love with your job or company? Will you have to take a new job that you are not super passionate about just because you need the money to maintain your current lifestyle?

Know Where You Stand Financially

- Have a financial plan. Document your goals and review and refine them annually at least. When you have a major lifestyle change, including a new job, update your financial plan so that you know when to open the exit door and jump if the going gets too tough. Some of the best moments I've seen clients experience are when they can go to work each day, knowing they don't need their current jobs to be OK financially.

Write down your own coaching tips here.

_____

_____

_____

_____

_____

_____

_____

_____

_____

_____

_____

_____

_____

_____

_____

_____

_____

_____

_____

_____

Lisa L. Brown, CFP®, CIMA®, MBA

_____
_____
_____
_____
_____
_____
_____
_____
_____
_____
_____
_____
_____
_____
_____
_____
_____
_____
_____
_____
_____
_____
_____
_____
_____
_____
_____
_____
_____
_____

CHAPTER 5

Mentors—the Power to Raise You or Break You

All the women interviewed had people of significance who helped shape their careers. Not all of these mentors were good role models though. By definition, a mentor is a trusted counselor or guide. Many companies have built formal in-house mentoring programs that match senior leaders with rising talent. In other cases, the mentors are external coaches. Based on their experiences, many of these women agree that formal mentoring programs do not work when there is a forced match-up. However, when relationships can be formed organically but with a certain level of structure, they can be incredibly impactful to both the mentor and the mentee. Carmen shared, "Don't be so egotistical that you don't need a mentor. You need to hear the hard truth." Ashley agreed with the power of mentorship. "You can help someone avoid ruining their career with five minutes of good advice."

Kate recalled an important mentor early in her career. Kate was a new mom, had started a job as a senior buyer at a major university, asked questions in meetings, and raised her hand to volunteer. A mentor took her in, advising Kate to get more professional designations. When she did, this mentor showed up at her house one day with a bottle of champagne to celebrate. Kate was just pulling into her driveway with her husband and two children in her car, which did not have air conditioning. It was a reality check for Kate. She had accomplished something not only important to her but also recognized by others. Later in her career, when Kate was in her early fifties, she was laid off. A different female mentor entered her life at an important time—a trail angel. This mentor met with Kate every three weeks for seven months, opening doors for her and introducing her to people she wanted to meet. Due to the selfless efforts of this mentor, Kate went on to become the president of a division in her next role. Both of these mentors raised Kate up with time and words.

Ronna found investment banking to be the most interesting course that she took at Harvard Business School. She went to work at a large national investment firm in order to build their corporate derivative efforts in North America, Asia, Europe, and Latin America. Ultimately, she built this division to a $1 billion revenue-generating group. When the Great Recession happened, it was a scary time, especially in the financial services industry. Big companies were collapsing or being folded into other giants, and jobs were slashed. Ronna saw all her senior mentors leave. Now they were outside her company, rather than inside. This made her nervous, sensing a lack of senior support during a shaky time for the economy and her company. Ultimately, one of her mentors encouraged her to leave. She did and got herself back in investment banking at a senior level. When her sphere of influence moved, she moved with it.

A mentor and mentee relationship can have varying degrees

of influence. Mentors can be more of a sounding board or go in-depth, helping you set goals and holding you accountable to action items. They can also open doors for you. How do you know if the mentor model is a good fit for you? The following list includes some suggestions for what to look for in a mentor or mentorship program.

- Gender neutrality—a mentorship program should have both male and female mentors from different backgrounds. Brooklyn was so natural at connecting people and making introductions that a male mentor told her to monetize that ability to supplement her lifestyle while working in the nonprofit world. Brooklyn felt guilty trying to monetize her relationships but found herself living below the poverty line for two years. Thanks to this advice, she figured out how to turn her introductions into revenue and is now looking at a six- to seven-figure payout on one deal.
- Accessibility to the mentor—the higher up in the organization the mentor is, the harder it can be to get time with them. You should know when they are accessible. Ashley takes calls from her mentees between 6:30 and 7:30 a.m., when she's running on the treadmill.
- Willingness to be in the trenches with you—Isabel shared that her favorite mentor would go on big sales appointments with her.
- Diversity—Ashley shared that the best mentors are people who don't look like you.
- Mentors working in a different industry—Carol spent her career in the media industry, yet mentors younger talents who work in a variety of fields.
- Multiple mentors—the good mentors are often

overwhelmed with too many people asking for their counsel. Have more than one mentor.

- Personal board of directors—pull together a group of three to five people who you can call anytime. They should be people who can help you process making a change, not just help you to do better at your current job.
- Companies that support mentorships and personal development – these companies can help connect you with vetted leaders willing to mentor.

The next level up from mentorship is sponsorship—someone who will get you a seat at the table or pull you through the door they just opened for you. Sponsorship takes time and has to be earned. It requires a greater level of trust and confidence in you—the rising talent—as the sponsor is generously sharing a slice of their credibility pie with you. A sponsorship can be unspoken. Whereas you might ask someone to invest time in being your mentor, you don't ask someone to stake their reputation on your performance and become your sponsor. Build the relationship. Prove yourself. Have energy and be open to learn from your potential sponsor. And it certainly doesn't hurt to take appropriate actions to make them look good too!

Sponsorships, like mentorships, can have benefits to both parties. Sponsors may be at points in their careers where they are more focused on their legacies than their individual performances. To the sponsor, success is helping someone else along. Early in her career, April had a great male mentor who became her sponsor. He "pushed aside barriers" for her. Her employer had no female officers at the time. Her mentor knew she'd be successful and wanted to make certain of this after he was gone. This is one piece of advice he gave her early on: "You are young, and you are female. So get over it and prove them with your confidence." She did over and over again.

The Power to Break You

Mentors have the power to make you or break you. Margaret initially thought she was fortunate to have a male boss who became her mentor. He took her under his wing and appeared to be positioning her to take over his job one day. What an honor! When this man took a role in a different division to keep advancing his career, he gave Margaret all the groups that he had been managing. When a different colleague of Margaret's thought so much of her that he told her former boss she could be the chief technology officer (CTO) one day, that compliment was like a nail in Margaret's coffin. That's when the floor started to fall from beneath Margaret's feet. Turns out, her former boss and mentor had always had his eye on the CTO role. Margaret was now viewed as competition. Their relationship became antagonistic. She was receiving no support from him and other leaders were seeing what was happening. In an attempt to protect Margaret, the current CTO assigned her to an overseas role. Margaret describes her time dealing with her former boss and mentor as "life changing" and it "ruined my career." Still to this day it's very difficult for Margaret to talk about her experience with this mentor.

While there are plenty of female professionals who desire to uplift the next generation of women—including every single one who contributed to this book—that's not always the case. Women have to watch out for other women at times. Virginia worked for a woman and thought she'd be a strong advocate for Virginia since they were both females. But this female boss shamed Virginia for asking questions. The advice Virginia received was "don't be so bubbly, tone yourself down, and figure out the job on your own." The lesson here is don't assume someone will be your mentor or be supportive of you simply because they are the same gender as you, or are in a position of authority. You need to carefully select your mentor as much as they need to carefully select you.

Finally, while you are looking for or developing a mentorship relationship, be on the lookout for your trail angels. Because of the trail angels Elizabeth has had in her life, she believes that some part of your life should always be wrapped around service to others or your community. "Reach behind and pull someone up," she shared. "If you need to, get behind them and push." Keep your eyes open for the people pushing you in a new direction. And when you arrive, invest your time in others to pay it forward.

CHAPTER 6

Am I Successful?

Very few women who I interviewed directly answered yes when asked if they considered themselves successful. Most were hesitant to claim that victory. They either didn't view success as measurable or were too humble to admit it. I do think that's common among the women in my circles who I consider successful—they are hesitant to own it. Perhaps that's another difference between men and women. Even if you don't express your happiness with your current professional status, be sure you're not being held back from trying new things, going after what you want, or speaking up for yourself. You've got this.

Success is squiggly, as Gia will tell you. She used to have annual personal goals and some career goals that she would regularly review. However, she never truly defined her career goals. Gia couldn't say if she had achieved her career goals, as they couldn't be measured. That's true for any goal. If you don't document your goals, make them measurable, or review your progress, you can't be certain they've been achieved. Gia is confident in her top two professional strengths: achievement and helpfulness. That's how she thinks about being successful.

Ashley feels like it's taken her fifty years to find confidence in herself. She always used to worry about job security, if someone would hire her, and if she'd be able to do something she enjoyed. Ashley had jobs where others thought she was more successful than she felt. She first recalled feeling successful when she was an officer at a pharmaceutical company, with over four hundred people reporting to her across the globe. In corporate America, success is delivering results and managing relationships. While at times she'd give herself an A+ for delivering results, she reported an F for networking. Yet relationships are key everywhere. Ashley agrees that people make decisions based on who they are familiar and comfortable with and who they trust. Then there was the time when she overheard a woman say, "Ashley is at *this* baby shower," like she was a big deal, rather than a regular co-worker in attendance. Perhaps notoriety is also a way to measure success.

Elizabeth describes success as an ever-evolving comfort with yourself—being comfortable in your own skin. Once Elizabeth became comfortable with her level of accomplishments, she decided to retire. Her husband had to help her get to this point, reminding her of the number of students she'd impacted. She had recently been recognized with a prestigious award for excellence in teaching that was voted on by her colleagues, current students, and alumni. It can take others recognizing the impact you've made before you allow yourself to see it and own it.

Being in her forties, Claire feels she has surpassed where she ever thought she'd be at this point in her career, as measured by the size of her clients and the status at her firm. She's recently become a TV personality, regularly interviewed for her expertise. To become successful, Claire had to learn that her activities needed to be the focus, not what the end result would look like. Making ten calls a day, every day, for five days a week to build your book of clients—those are the activities. The end result is a book of revenue worth seven figures after two years of those consistent activities. At the beginning of her career, she worked twelve to fourteen hours a day, including on the weekends. Now, after fifteen years in her industry, she works six to eight hours a day and can spend her workday doing the activities she loves, such as networking for new clients.

As a fifty-year-old woman, Josephine realizes that she is "not making a career anymore." She doesn't spend her days trying to figure out how to be successful. Looking ahead, she prefers to only do work that she enjoys, such as being a business advisor—the calm in the storm—or diving into a new job with a vengeance. But only if she really likes the people.

While working at her Fortune 500 company in the 1980s, Margaret broke the glass ceiling every step of the way. "I should have a headache!" she declared. She was invited to special lunches with the C-suite, even though her role wasn't typically on the invite list. She was the first woman to become a director and a first vice president and the first woman to lead the European sector. Looking back as a retiree, she acknowledges that she was successful. But if you were once a success, will you always be a success? Once Margaret left corporate America, several friends encouraged her to pursue consulting, public speaking and writing opportunities given her strong and vast corporate experience. Margaret did publish a book that was well received, but it did not give her the traction she expected for consulting and speaking gigs. Yet Margaret learned to define success differently. Now it is about accepting life as it manifests itself, embracing her art and home roles and most importantly, living in the moment. "Life is what comes to you" and "rebelling against it is only a way of finding frustration" shares Margaret.

The first time Ann felt successful was eight years ago, when she was fifty. The top twelve people at her Fortune 500 company were considered the leadership team. At the first meeting that she joined, she asked herself, "Do I belong here?" Of those twelve people, three were women. It took Ann thirty years of working at this same company before she earned her spot on the leadership team. Now Ann sees rising stars at companies who get involved in different projects and have unique levels of drive. But having young children can change your track. One young female with high potential would be capable of filling Ann's role one day, but she does not want to move. As a result, her career could be limited. Ann talks a lot with younger, talented individuals about their career trajectories. These days, her concern is that young people won't be patient enough to stay at a company. They'll get frustrated and leave too soon. Loyalty to an organization is different today.

Women typically aren't boastful about their success. They may feel proud of themselves inwardly before they express it. What will it take for you to feel successful? What steps are you taking to get there?

CHAPTER 7

Diversity and Discrimination

If there is one topic that is jaw-dropping to me from my interviews of these successful women, it is the wide-spread workplace discrimination against women that has happened and continues to happen. Under federal law, treating an employee differently or unfairly based on their gender is illegal. Title VII of the Civil Rights Act of 1964 outlawed gender discrimination, yet it continues to happen. A CareerBuilder survey found that 72 percent of victims of sexual discrimination continue to keep quiet for fear of reprisal from their employers.[2] All these stories of discrimination have occurred in the last few decades; we're not talking about the 1960s here.

Let's face it. During our careers, gender discrimination will likely keep happening, whether it be to us or those around us. Like most negative experiences, it's about how you react and

---

[2] Bryan Robinson, "Gender Discrimination Is Still Alive and Well in the Workplace in 2021," *Forbes*, February 15, 2021, https://www.forbes.com/sites/bryanrobinson/2021/02/15/gender-discrimination-is-still-alive-and-well-in-the-workplace-in-2021/?sh=afc9ff97f1c9.

move forward, as all these women have. It's up to each of us to not only be supportive of other women who face discrimination but also speak up for them when they cannot or will not. If you find yourself in a situation similar to the women in this chapter, I hope you find the strength and wisdom to address the issue, learn from it, and forge ahead stronger. As you'll also see, you can use your gender to your advantage.

Age Discrimination

The *Forbes* article "Gender Discrimination Is Still Alive and Well in the Workplace in 2021" featured a story about a highly qualified female faculty member at a university who was denied her tenure and promotion. The discussion around the dean's conference table went like this: "She's an old maid. Wonder why she's never been married?"[2] This woman was fired from her position, despite the fact that the prominent university clearly stated it did not discriminate on the basis of gender.

Krista experienced age discrimination early in her career, when a male boss said to her, "You are too young to be the head of HR." Yet four years after graduating college, she became the director of compensation and, thirteen years after that, earned the position of principal for the talent department of a national consulting firm. Krista might not have had a boss who could see past her age, but that didn't stop her from achieving larger roles with more responsibility. Today, she's the senior vice president of an IT services and consulting firm.

Sexual Discrimination

Early in Josephine's career, she gave a presentation to a group of company leaders. She wore a skirt that went to her knees and a contoured jacket. She saw the CEO looking her up and down the entire time she was speaking, and it threw her off balance. Josephine's takeaway was that she "should have worn pants."

Carol shared that a lot of her career was spent forcing people to respect her brains, not her looks. As a result, she always focused on dressing appropriately. Her definition of that included no loud jewelry or anything she felt would be distracting.

Gender Identity and Sexual Orientation Discrimination

Gender identity and sexual orientation are other examples of discrimination impacting women today. During the pandemic, Maya was handling most of her meetings via Zoom and included the she/her pronouns on her name tag. When a higher-level male colleague asked her about her pronouns, he commented, "I'm not confused about who I am or what I am." Maya's heart was racing. She felt embarrassed. The company she worked for proclaimed that they promoted inclusiveness, but this colleague clearly did not support the company's stated policy. She messaged him about his comment but never heard back. Maya wished she had been more direct with him about how she felt. If he said that to her face, what was being said about her behind her back?

Maya also faced a challenging situation from a male client regarding her sexual orientation. This client was not happy that his advisor had left or that Maya, a "lower-level person", was assigned to service his account. When getting to know one another, the client asked Maya if she was married. Maya confirmed that she was engaged. The client asked if she was engaged to a man or a woman, so Maya lied, saying she was engaged to a man. The client responded, "Oh good, because I hate that sexual sh*t."

When Maya shared this experience with her boss, he asked, "Oh, do you want us to do something about this?" Maya was thirty-four years old and worried about being labeled a tattletale. She knew speaking up could hurt her career. She met with this client several times after the incident and retained him as a customer, but she ultimately left the company, as she couldn't bear having to come out to him and the other 180 clients she worked with. Looking back at this incident, Maya's advice is to confront the person and then tell your senior leader. Educate the person who wronged you about how they made you feel. All her life, it was engrained in her not to be confrontational. But these issues do need to be met head-on.

Quinn, known as "Jake" at the time, first realized that she was uncomfortable with her male gender at the age of four or five. It took her over four decades to come out as female. At age twenty-one, she started working for a large investment company and spent many years on the trading desk, enjoying great success. She wanted to play the part, so she bought books on what the ideal man should look and dress like—tall, brown hair, knowledgeable and resembling Clark Kent. This persona helped open up many career opportunities for "Jake," spanning from mutual fund distribution to marketing and public speaking.

When Quinn began her transition from a man to a woman, she was working at a large financial company that internally marketed itself as not having to solicit clients. Due to their prestige, clients came to them. About seven months into her transition, she was starting to look more like a woman but still wore men's suits. The firm began questioning who they had hired. She quit, and the general manager told her they were going to fire her anyway. Later, while applying at another firm as a transgender woman, she was told, "Someone, somewhere, will say something stupid, and our company doesn't want to take on that risk."

Three years into her transition, Quinn started her own financial planning firm. When calling on old clients, she found that the male clients wouldn't return her calls. Many of her former female clients wouldn't come on board either. As a transwoman, Quinn has developed several conclusions:

1. Transwomen are unique in that they are the only ones who can confirm sexism exists.
2. On average, men treat women worse than women treat men when they are the only one of their gender in the room.
3. The discrimination that Quinn has faced in her recent career journey is more about being a woman than about being transgender.

Race Discrimination

"All the time" was Ashley's response when I asked if she'd ever faced discrimination in the workplace. About twenty years ago, Ashley was an executive vice president of marketing. A long-time agency partner of her employer told her that they would not take orders from "a little black girl" and turned her away. Fortunately, she told her boss, who then promptly ended the relationship with this agency partner. A few years ago, Ashley was running a large division for a global company and was told by a senior officer, "You're so good—so smart. You just don't look the part. I don't think people will be comfortable with you."

As Elizabeth commented on race discrimination, "It's your problem, not mine. My job is to get people to know me personally."

At age thirty-four, Eva was prepared to present a business plan at a meeting that people flew in from around the world to attend. Her boss told her, "You need to move. I can't have two black people sitting next to one another here." The only open seat was in the back of the room. Her boss then raised his voice to her. "Just move, dammit!" Eva wanted to quit her job at that moment. She told another superior what had happened, and he encouraged her to speak with her boss. She did, and they spent the entire day talking it out. Eva did not quit and ultimately earned a role in the C-suite at that company. Another impactful comment Eva shared regarding her race is she avoids country clubs, as they're always reminders to her that she's "different," meaning she's not a white man or white woman.

Gender Discrimination

Many of the women in this book feel there is a stereotype about how pretty or thin a woman needs to be in order to get ahead in the workplace. Several also feel that gender can and should be used to their advantage. Amelia's perspective is that beauty can be a deterrent for a woman. As a woman, you lose credibility if you are too attractive, but for men, it's not possible to be too attractive. However, Carol believes that successful women in corporate America are also attractive, especially women in sales. She shared a story with me about a 295-pound woman in San Diego who lost one hundred pounds and received four promotions within a year of dropping the weight. "A man can get fat and ugly, and nobody cares," shared Ashley. "Women can't be fat and ugly in corporate America." She feels like she needs to be thin and perfectly polished, hence her daily ritual on the treadmill.

April worked for a southern company and experienced the "good ole boys' club" mentality. When it came to hiring, her male boss wanted "one of their own." April did not think this male candidate was the right fit. She spoke up but ultimately was not heard. When this new hire did not work out, her boss came back to her and said, "I'll never not listen to you again."

Before her transition, Quinn recalled a business trip to Las Vegas that the sales manager only invited men on. Since this sales manager defined so many people's success, Quinn knew that she needed to attend the Vegas trip, but she also realized that women would never be successful in any sales roles there. At another large investment firm, she found that all the men were on the trading side, and all the women were in marketing. As a male at the time, she felt it was to her advantage to be the only male in marketing, but the women hated her for entering their space. As a male, she experienced gender discrimination from women. In 2020, around the time of the George Floyd incident, the CEO of Quinn's wealth management company sent the employees an email about how proud he was of their firm's diversity. Per Quinn, the only diversity at the company was in the mailroom. She called the CEO and commented that of the twenty-eight salespeople there, twenty-seven were white men, and they were the ones who made all the money. She was fired four days later.

Early in Krista's health-care career, she felt discriminated against because she wasn't "an old white guy who grew the business." But gender discrimination isn't always about how men treat women. It's also how women treat other women. In the last decade, Krista has experienced more discrimination from women than men. She has had some terrible female bosses and has found women trying to figuratively slit each other's throats. At upper levels, Krista sees women as very competitive, trying to move each other out of the way while thinking, "If there can only be one, I want it to be me." Now it's the men she's surrounded by who are most supportive of her. "Women hold grudges; men don't."

As Madeline Albright said in 2016, "There's a special place in hell for women who don't help each other!"

Bullying

Bullying happens in the workplace. If this impacts you, it's a critical time to have an ally. Bullies prey on people who are vulnerable. If you are being bullied like April was, her advice is to not panic. Fear can shut you down. Take careful notes, documenting what is happening. The bully will try to make you feel like you are crazy, but if you write down your experiences, you'll see that's not the case. Also, an outside coach or counselor can become your ally and provide you with a fresh perspective on how to handle the situation. In April's case, the person bullying her was a senior male leader in the company. April was in a senior HR role and had confidence in the company's need to create a certain business partner role. The male leader disagreed and told her that if she didn't stop pushing for this new role, her career trajectory would go downhill. While April tried to deal with this male leader one-on-one, he wouldn't stand down. She was taking notes on their conversations right in front of him. Finally, she had to take the documented situation a step above him, and the male leader was eventually removed as her boss and relieved of all his leadership responsibilities. She stood up to the bully, but it took courage.

Several years ago, Kate joined a team of male vice presidents who had worked together for a long time. They did not accept her as part of their VP team, creating a narrative that the team did not like her. During this time Kate was winning one of the highest leadership awards in her company. Their boss had a high level of trust in Kate, which created jealousy among the men. Things blew up, and ultimately, the CEO of their $4 billion company got involved. Kate tried to hold herself to the highest level of integrity throughout this ordeal, even offering to have calls or dinner with these men in order to work through their issues, but they cancelled on her. The male VPs were not the only men that created a challenging work environment for Kate. Two other difficult men directly reported to Kate. She led these two direct reports through an industry leading quality management certification process, making a major impact on the business and their careers. Of this group of men, only one is left, and she's still trying to "earn it" with him. Fortunately, her boss has been rock solid with her throughout this ordeal, or else she would have resigned.

Can Being Different Work to Your Advantage?

Amelia grew up in Ireland and has an Irish accent. In the US, she didn't sound or look like everyone else in meetings. Rather than feeling awkward in business meetings, Amelia decided to use that to her advantage and was more comfortable speaking up as a result. Ann, on the other hand, felt a bias against her when doing business in foreign countries. When she was in Poland, she always had a translator with her. Many people in the room thought Ann was the translator, not the person there to sign the contract, because she was female. German businessmen also often tried to dismiss her. Ann believes that she was able to get these foreign men to do business with her because of the powerful global brand she worked for.

Fortunately, Ronna had a supportive employer. One day a group of Korean businessmen exclaimed, "She is Korean, and no Korean woman is allowed in the meeting." Her male boss replied, "If she can't come, our company will go home." Ronna was allowed in the meeting; however, nobody looked at her the entire time. It felt like the worst meeting of her professional life. Fifteen years later, she learned that those Korean businessmen applauded her after the meeting, asking "How come Korean women only serve coffee?" That group of businessmen ended up launching an initiative to bring women into finance in Korea.

Darlene started her career in the construction industry, a male-dominated field. The fact that she was a minority wasn't a factor in her career path. In fact, she had a few female leaders to look up to early on. A few men in the field didn't want to take direction from Darlene since she was female, but she learned to ask questions that opened up conversation, as people like to talk about themselves. Being female in a male-dominated business isn't easy, but it can become your main advantage.

CHAPTER 8

Marriage, Divorce, and Health Hiccups

Friends was a very popular show when many of the women featured in this book were beginning their career journeys. Little did they know The Rembrandts line in the show's theme song—"so no one told you life was gonna be this way"—would ring so true. As a working woman, you balance the needs of so many people: family, colleagues, bosses, and friends. It can be easy to take for granted time with your loved ones when your work family is in constant need of your time, but your family and friends are the ones who will be there to pick you up off the ground when you stumble.

Judy was married for twenty-four years. During that time, her husband struggled with addiction but eventually got healed through a faith-based recovery program. While they were living in Las Vegas, he developed a brain tumor in an area that was hard to reach. He had three operations in five years. His sight was impacted, and after the third surgery, he began having seizures in the ICU. Living in a vegetative state, he never woke up or moved following the last surgery. After waiting three grueling weeks in the ICU for some change, the family had to make the decision to remove life support. Her husband passed away. The experience of healing from multiple life trials strengthened Judy's faith, and she now speaks to groups about giving hope through healing and moving forward and out of a state of emotional paralysis. She is the one who is there to help pick people up off the ground.

Carmen has been married for forty years. Her advice is to "marry the right person." This changes the options you have in your career. Find someone who is supportive and understanding and who looks at your career. Ashley agrees. Find a life partner if you are getting married—someone who stands behind you 100 percent and who will protect your personal time. "When your partner puts their arms around you after a tough day, it should feel magical," shared Ashley.

Both Darlene and her husband were on solid career trajectories when they started a family. When their first baby was born, nobody at Darlene's company had ever worked part-time. She took eight months off, unpaid, and became one of the first people in the Atlanta office to work part-time. Darlene wanted to feel like a full-time mom and a full-time employee, and she tried so hard to make it work. Then her husband's career took off. Flip-flopping, Darlene's career took off thereafter, which included a travel schedule. Her husband subsequently decided to take a different role in order to accommodate her schedule. That was ten years ago, and they still ask each other, "Are you still happy? Do you like your role?" They know this is a balancing act and want to ensure the scale doesn't become too tipped or that neither one of their senses of happiness and fulfillment are sacrificed.

As a CEO and COO, Leia has no balance in her life when she is working. Her passion is fixing organizations that are underperforming. Given this fast pace and the sacrifices she makes when she works, Leia takes a six-to-twelve-month break every three to five years. Right now, she is in her off-ramp period. When she does work, her son and husband know she's all in on work. Her son once told her, "I think Dad should work now, and you should stay home." That's not the arrangement they have. Leia and her husband were married for twelve years before having their son. Her husband was in sales, in the technology field. When their son was born, they agreed that a parent would always be home for breakfast and dinner. Her husband made that commitment and became the full-time parent. Leia knows that if her husband were as committed to his career as she has been, Leia would not have taken this path. Her husband continues to be a strong support system for Leia, encouraging her to take new jobs and move on when it feels right.

Trisha is the career-driven one in her relationship. Her husband is in physical therapy, but Trisha's career comes first, including when deciding if they will move to a new state. Trisha encourages women to be selfish with what they want. "We prioritize being a wife and mother and feel guilty when we put our career first." Trisha wants women to feel permitted to get the big job, knowing they'll have to put in the hours. "If you have joy at work, you'll do better in all of your other roles."

We're not all fortunate enough to have a partner who puts us first. Margaret and her husband were working for the same company. There were times when she held a more senior role than her husband, including a period when he reported to her. During this time, her husband would often not attend the department meetings Margaret was leading. When he did attend, her husband would openly provide his negative feedback such as "that doesn't make sense" or "that's stupid". Margaret would ignore her husband when he wasn't being supportive.

Marriage and Finances

Growing up, Gia's father was not very present. His dream was to own a country store, and he bought one when Gia was in her teens. Unfortunately, he did not have much business sense, and after divorcing from Gia's mom, he went bankrupt. Gia's mom worked three jobs to make ends meet for her three daughters. The mantra that Gia learned from her parents was "whatever you want, we'll figure it out later." This lesson got Gia into some tough financial situations after college. She did not realize that her parents had borrowed all the money for her to attend college, and she didn't understand what it meant to have student loans, nor did she have strategies for paying them off. Right before Gia got married, she had a six-figure student loan balance. She and her husband almost didn't get married because of her debt.

Judy had a marketing consulting business while her husband was on 100% commission in commercial real estate in Las Vegas when the market crashed in 2008. Not reducing their overhead in optimism that his business would rebound (which it did not) sent them in a financial spiral, blazing through savings and relying too heavily on credit to survive. The family had additional debt from his previous business and the debt, plus lack of income, forced a decision to declare bankruptcy. They relocated with their two children to a more corporate market and had to completely rebuild financially as a family.

As Trisha moved up the corporate ladder, she started spending more money, since she perceived people expected that of her. Then she found herself in debt. Her husband was enjoying the bigger lifestyle, which involved having more flashy things. But things didn't bring Trisha joy. Trisha knew she had to turn this around, and she did. They will be paying off their house in two years. Trisha shared, "Financial freedom is huge." It gives you the flexibility to stay in your current job or leave, change careers or industries, take some calculated risks, and have more peace in your marriage.

Ashley spent decades working her tail off in corporate America. She recently took a break and shared, "It's magical to get to a place when you can afford to take a pause." This is especially true now that Ashley's children are grown, and she has time to focus on herself.

Divorce

According to a 2020 *Business Insider* feature, research conducted by a professor at Stockholm University concluded that women who received big promotions were more likely to get divorced, and women were twice as likely as men to get divorced three years after a CEO-level promotion. Divorce rates increased for females who earned top jobs in politics as well as for female doctors and police officers. In this study, researchers also found that most successful women who divorced had children; however, in many cases, those children were grown and out of the house at the time of the divorce.[3] Divorce is a reality for working women, especially as they climb higher and higher.

Kate got divorced when her children were eight and ten. As

---

[3] Valerie H. Tocci, "Research Shows that More Women Are Likely to Get Divorced Shortly After a Promotion—and That's Not a Bad Thing," *Business Insider*, February 19, 2020, https://www.businessinsider.com/research-shows-women-more-likely-get-divorced-after-promotion-2020-2?amp.

a single mother living with both her children, she had to hire nannies and au pairs since she had to jump on airplanes in a heartbeat for work. Her son was in middle school and became very angry about the divorce. One day, Kate called her ex-husband and made arrangements for their son to live with him in a different city. The tug and pull that this caused on Kate's heart led her to move closer to her ex-husband, taking her off the promotion track. One fear that Kate had was financial— as a single mom, it was all on her to ensure she had enough money. Kate had always been disciplined about savings with the goal to retire at sixty. Then she found herself out of work for seven months. When she was unemployed, she went after opportunities like it was her job. She knew nobody was there to catch her. Kate's advice is to make sure you are able to take financial bumps in your life. Divorce or unemployment can be one of those financial bumps.

When Brooklyn was twenty-five and making a six-figure income, life was exciting. She got used to the high-flying lifestyle. But then, at age four, her daughter received a cancer diagnosis, was in hospice, and almost passed away. Hospice was a wake-up call for Brooklyn. While in sales, she was working all the time and had no time for her children or husband. Her marriage was falling apart. Brooklyn took a pay cut of over $100,000 and pivoted into the nonprofit world. She has never been happier. Her significantly lower income was a financial blessing, as the $1.2 million medical bill racked up when her daughter was in the ICU was covered by the state. Ultimately, Brooklyn's marriage ended, but her children told her they were proud of her for working in the nonprofit world. They want to be just like her, sharing a passion with a purpose.

Health Hiccups

Tomorrow is not promised to any of us. We don't know if we'll still be able to run at top speed professionally or personally. As women, we tend to put everyone else's needs first, not putting ourselves at the top of our priority lists. Yet if we are not functioning at 100 percent, we can't deliver 100 percent to those who need results from us.

Lucy thrived in a fast-paced environment, doing lots of volunteer work and attending networking events in the evening. About a year before her diagnosis of Parkinson's disease, she suddenly found herself anxious and stressed. She would fall asleep on her way home from work and napped in her car in the parking lot during the day. Lucy was thirty-four years old and shouldn't have felt this tired. She spent the first eighteen months after her diagnosis thinking about her disease every day. Then she realized that her life was not over, and she had to live in the present. Eventually, Lucy decided to slow down. She shifted to working thirty hours per week and put herself ahead of her career. Six months after slowing down at work, Lucy's husband noticed that she didn't have as many symptoms, which she attributed to having less work stress in her life. If you are diagnosed with an illness or disease that will inhibit you from functioning at 100 percent, Lucy's advice is to take it day by day and go with the flow more. Tell your employer and others about your needs and how you'd like their help as you move forward. If necessary, hire an attorney who can help you understand your rights as an employee. Bring awareness to your health situation.

After being encouraged to take a sales role in her early thirties, Isabel had the most successful year of her career. Achieving a spot in the President's Club allowed her to choose her next career path, as it was a powerful title to have on her resume. However, Isabel felt the pressure to achieve a spot in the President's Club the next year and found herself exhausted. Her boss and mentor encouraged her to take a new role, and she agreed. The morning that Isabel was to start her new role in the same organization, she started sweating while still at home. Dizziness set in, and her throat closed up. Isabel called 911. At thirty-four, she suffered a stroke. After being hospitalized, Isabel lost her left peripheral vision and had to learn how to walk again by going to rehab. Swallowing was difficult; she lived on applesauce and soft foods for several months. Then cognitive issues set in. Eighteen months after having her stroke, Isabel hired a life coach, and that changed her trajectory. She left sales and got into the coaching business herself, becoming a certified life coach in 2021. Instead of asking herself why this happened to her, she learned to question *why not*. Isabel's mother had passed away at age thirty-four. Her mom didn't make it, but Isabel did.

CHAPTER 9

Parenting and Off-Ramping

Anyone reading this who is a mother knows the phrase "mommy guilt." According to Sophia, "the guilt of working moms never stops." Knowing that your job as a parent is to launch your kids becomes hard when you aren't with them all the time. Time seems too short. But there is a difference between caregiving and missing your children's important activities. Sophia remembers being asked to show her ID at daycare when picking up her children, for she rarely was the one to do the drop-offs and pickups. When her children were in high school, she was traveling a lot for work, so she had a pact with her children. "Tell me when it's nonnegotiable to be there. If it's important to them I attend, I will."

Darlene's children are pretty independent and successful. They didn't freak out if both of their parents weren't at each activity. Darlene advised, "You don't have to be at everything. But when you say you're going to be somewhere, you better show up."

Being surrounded by stay-at-home moms when she was building her career, Carol once asked her children's school counselor if she was there enough. The counselor responded, "You weren't always here, but you were here when it was appropriate. A lot of moms were here too much." As working women, we don't often think about that angle, but being too present is not a good thing.

Many working moms likely contemplate quitting their jobs and becoming full-time parents at some point. According to a 2019 study by the American Management Association, family pull factors remain the top reason for career downshifting, and 69 percent of women said they would not have off-ramped if their companies had offered flexible work options such as reduced-hour schedules, job sharing, part-time career tracks, or short unpaid sabbaticals. The average length of an off-ramp is 2.7 years. Seventy-three percent of women who try to return to the workforce after a voluntary timeout to care for children or other reasons have trouble finding a job. Those who do find a job report a 16 percent reduction in earning power, and over 25 percent report a decrease in their management responsibilities. Off-ramping is a major decision with potentially long-term career implications.[4]

Ashley contemplated quitting her job. At the time, she had three children—ages four, two, and an infant. Some days she felt like the worst mom ever, feeding her kids hot dogs for dinner. It was her mother-in-law who challenged her. "You love what you do. What are you going to do all day?" Now, Ashley would say that her kids see her as the best mom ever. She takes her experience as a young mother and tries to make the path easier for those women coming after her. During the early stages of COVID-19, Ashley would tell the working

[4] American Management Association staff, "Time Outs Take an Increasing Toll on Women's Careers," January 24, 2019, https://www.amanet.org/articles/time-outs-take-an-increasing-toll-on-women-s-careers/.

moms on her team to take time each day to fully focus on their children. Put your phone away and stop sending emails. This is an example of how an employer can avoid losing out on the valuable contributions of women, who represent 58 percent of the highly credentialed pool.[5]

Working in the male-dominated financial services industry, Ronna was fortunate enough to work for a boss who said, "Prioritize your child, so you don't resent this company." Ronna would take breast milk to work and store it in the refrigerator. The company built systems for her upon her return to work that she is pleased are still in place today. Ronna always had hired help; sometimes two nannies worked for her. Her life was never balanced, but she didn't feel rushed to get home from work, knowing she had caregivers for her son. She arranged her business travel so she never missed her son's doctor appointments or school plays.

When Virginia was in corporate America, she felt shunned for setting personal boundaries. Early in her career, she had no boundaries. Becoming an entrepreneur forced a change in her, and now Virginia will say no to attending any evening event on a night when she has her daughter at home. The following is one of my favorite lines: "No is a complete sentence."

Amelia worried about her kids all the time when they were growing up. Her advice to younger moms is to not worry. Her children turned out great, even though she worked a lot of hours during their childhoods. She often heard them say, "I don't want a job like yours where you're on the phone the entire time. Why am I the only kid whose dad picks them up from school?" Women will continue to worry about their families, kids, and careers. This won't stop. But learning how to keep life in perspective and focus on what matters most can help get you through the tough days.

---

[5] American Management Association staff, "Time Outs."

Gia, on the other hand, did off-ramp. Her sabbatical happened quickly, prompted by their nanny quitting. "If kid care goes to crap, it severely impacts your working situation," said Gia. She was determined not to find another nanny outside their network—which would have been their tenth—to care for her children while she and her husband juggled demanding full-time careers. Gia either needed to find a nanny in their network or realize the universe was telling her something. Well, both happened. A family friend stepped in to help for six months, allowing Gia to slow down gradually. Knowing she would leave her job, Gia spent time figuring out what she wanted to do next. A list of all the things she wanted to get done around the house evolved. She also enlisted an executive coach to help her plan her transition and how she would spend her time. During her final months at work, her assistant carved off "think time" on Gia's calendar, so she had business hours to think about what to do with herself next. She also spent a lot of time talking with other people who had taken sabbaticals.

Once her sabbatical began, Gia realized just how fast those seven hours that your children are in school go by! When sitting in the carpool line, her nose was in a book. She focused on her children's needs, such as knocking out her son's bedwetting problem over four weeks. Sometimes, if she woke up and didn't feel good, she'd sit on the couch and read. Before, she'd trudge through in order to get to work. There became very few days when Gia felt guilty that she didn't accomplish anything. No longer was she seeking self-validation from her job. She is getting her validation elsewhere. As a result of her sabbatical, she now has a new respect for full-time mothers.

Over the last ten years, the things that Kirstin finds nonnegotiable have changed. Taking her children to school each day was important; it became the only time her teenage son would talk with her. And Josephine advises that younger mothers not compromise their children or family for their work. That's great advice to wrap up this chapter.

CHAPTER 10

Nonnegotiables

The following are the top activities that these successful women insist upon in order to stay fulfilled and take care of themselves. They are the keys to success! A special thanks to fifteen-year-old Leigh Namgung who sketched these images to enhance this chapter.

1. Meditate

2. Pray

3. Express gratitude

4. Take your children to school

5. Exercise

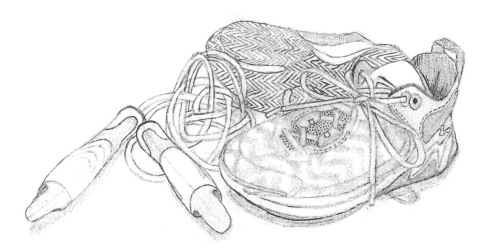

6. Take one hour for yourself every day

7. Be home for dinner whenever you are not traveling

8. Write a to-do list and check things off

9. Take vacations, including one-on-one trips with your children

10. Know where you stand financially

ABOUT THE AUTHOR

As a strategic leader, Lisa Brown has spent her entire career in wealth management, counseling hundreds of corporate executives through life and financial transitions. She regularly speaks at women's affinity groups across corporate America and has been featured in *The New York Times, The Wall Street Journal, CNBC.com, Yahoo! Finance,* and many other media outlets.

Lisa is the author of *Girl Talk, Money Talk: The Smart Girl's Guide to Money After College* and *Girl Talk, Money Talk II: Financially Fit and Fabulous in Your 40s and 50s.* Learn more at www.girltalkmoneytalk.com.

She is active on nonprofit boards and committees, serving families, children, and pets experiencing homelessness. Lisa is married and lives in the suburbs of Atlanta with her husband and three children, including a set of twins, and her corgi.

Printed in the United States
by Baker & Taylor Publisher Services